50

THINGS YOU SHOULD KNOW ABOUT

WILD WEATHER

by Anna Claybourne

Publisher: Maxime Boucknooghe
Editorial Director: Victoria Garrard
Art Director: Laura Roberts-Jensen
Project Editor: Sophie Hallam
Consultant: Dave Hawksett
Designed, edited and picture researched by: Starry Dog Books Ltd

Copyright © QED Publishing 2015

First published in the UK in 2015 by
QED Publishing
Part of The Quarto Group
The Old Brewery,
6 Blundell Street,
London, N7 9BH

www.qed-publishing.co.uk

A catalogue record for this book is available from the British Library.

ISBN 978 1 78493 304 3

Printed in China

Words in **bold** are explained in the Glossary on page 78.

CONTENTS

INTRODUCTION

Global warming affects the entire planet and is changing our weather. Watch out for this global warming symbol throughout the book.

Humans have worked out how to control lots of things. We farm crops and animals, reshape the land and build giant towers and bridges. But one thing we have little control over is our world's wild weather. There's not much we can do to stop a downpour, prevent a lightning strike or change the path of a deadly, roaring hurricane. We are at the weather's mercy!

▲ Locals try to clear a road during a powerful typhoon in Zhanjiang, China.

▲ A 'supercell' storm cloud such as this one in Nebraska, United States, can spawn deadly tornadoes.

WEIRD WEATHER

Once in a while, the weather puts on amazing displays for us. It even creates sights so strange we can't believe our eyes. You might see clouds that look like flying saucers, red rain or even a fish falling from the sky (see pages 37 and 62–63)!

WHEN WEATHER TURNS WILD

Weather doesn't always cause problems. Sometimes it's perfect! Sometimes it's annoying, but harmless. But, occasionally, extreme and scary weather conditions come along. Powerful winds, lightning strikes, heatwaves and ice storms can be dangerous, and even deadly. Extreme weather can lead to other disasters, too, such as floods, landslides, road accidents and electricity **blackouts**.

▼ *A summer thunderstorm puts on a stunning display of forked lightning over Tucson, Arizona, in the United States.*

▲ *Snowfall after a blizzard in New York City, United States, makes getting around difficult!*

▲ *Locals team up to stage a rescue after heavy rain causes a flood in the Philippines.*

What is weather?

Weather is what is going on in the **atmosphere** (the air around the Earth) at any moment – how cloudy, sunny, wet or dry it is. It can change a lot from day to day.

We enjoy blue skies when there are no clouds in the way.

Wind blows clouds along and can make the air feel colder.

When the temperature is colder, snow is more likely.

WATER, WIND AND WARMTH

Weather is made up of three main things:

 Water The air contains water in the form of **water vapour** (an invisible gas), clouds or fog. It can fall as rain, sleet, snow or hail.

 Air Air moving around the planet makes wind. Air pressure – the way air pushes down on our planet – also affects the weather.

 Temperature Is it hot or cold, or somewhere in between? Sunshine, the time of year and where the wind has come from all affect the temperature.

WEATHER OPPOSITES

Most weather is a mixture of several different conditions. Which of these would you use to describe the weather where you are today?

Cloudy ←→ Clear
or

Wet ←→ Dry
or

Cold ←→ Warm
or

Windy ←→ Calm
or

Clouds form from water droplets in the air.

◀ *Big mountains such as this one, Mount Rundle in Canada, have an effect on the weather as wind and clouds blow up and over them.*

Rainbows happen when sunshine bounces in and out of raindrops or mist.

Clouds block the sunshine, casting shadows.

The Earth's atmosphere
Weather happens in the atmosphere, the layer of gases around the Earth (see page 8).

Weather fronts
A weather **front** is the front edge of a moving mass of warm or cold air (see page 9).

Weather around the world
Different parts of our planet experience many different types of weather (see pages 10–11).

The Earth's atmosphere

Our planet, the Earth, is surrounded by a thin layer of air called the atmosphere. The air can heat up, cool down, move around and carry water. It also has a pushing force, called air pressure. Scientists divide the atmosphere into five layers. Most weather happens in the layer nearest the Earth's surface.

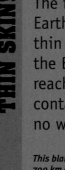

THIN SKIN!

The first four layers of the Earth's atmosphere form a thin blanket of gases around the Earth. The exosphere reaches out further, but it contains hardly any air and no weather.

This blanket is only 700 km deep – a tiny proportion of the Earth's diameter.

The Earth is 12,742 km across.

There is no weather on the Moon because it has almost no atmosphere.

Some satellites orbit in the exosphere, others in the thermosphere.

5 **EXOSPHERE**
700–10,000 km above the Earth's surface

Spacecraft orbit the Earth in the thermosphere.

THERMOSPHERE
80–700 km above the Earth's surface **4**

Most meteors (space rocks) burn up in the mesosphere.

MESOSPHERE
50–80 km above the Earth's surface **3**

WEATHER
....

The troposphere is where most of the Earth's weather happens. This is where the air is thickest.

STRATOSPHERE
12–50 km above the Earth's surface **2**

TROPOSPHERE
0–12 km above the Earth's surface **1**

Jet planes often fly up into the stratosphere, above the clouds.

Weather fronts

Weather forecasters often talk about 'fronts'. A weather front is a dividing line between two different blocks or masses of air. One air mass may be cold and dry, while another could be warm and damp.

ON THE MAP

On weather maps, cold fronts are shown as blue lines with triangles, and warm fronts are shown as red lines with half-circles.

3

▼ This bank of cloud is a cold front pushing against a mass of cloudless warm air.

Snow

High

▶ The pointy 'icicles' show which way the cold front is heading.

▲ The rounded half-circles indicating warm fronts look like little 'suns'.

Low

Rain

FRONTS

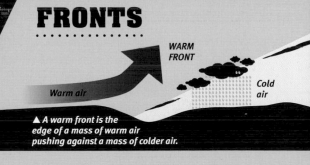

WARM FRONT

Warm air

Cold air

▲ A warm front is the edge of a mass of warm air pushing against a mass of colder air.

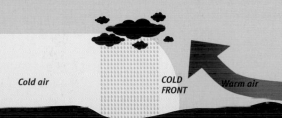

Cold air

COLD FRONT

Warm air

▲ A cold front is the edge of a mass of cold air pushing against a mass of warmer air.

STORMY WEATHER

Weather fronts can cause stormy and cloudy weather, as the air masses involved push each other out of the way. Warmer air usually gets pushed up. As it rises and cools, it usually forms clouds, which release rain.

Weather around the world

Weather conditions around the world vary a lot. This is mainly because some parts of the Earth get stronger sunshine than others, so they are warmer. The shapes of continents, oceans and mountains also affect the weather in different places.

WEATHER EVENTS

Some parts of the world have a weather pattern that affects them the same way every year. For example, monsoon winds bring heavy monsoon rains to parts of Africa and Asia in the summer.

▶ A tornado on the American plains in Tornado Alley.

TORNADO ALLEY

In spring and early summer, a tornado season brings a surge of tornadoes to an area known as Tornado Alley in the central part of the United States.

Tornado Alley

UNITED STATES

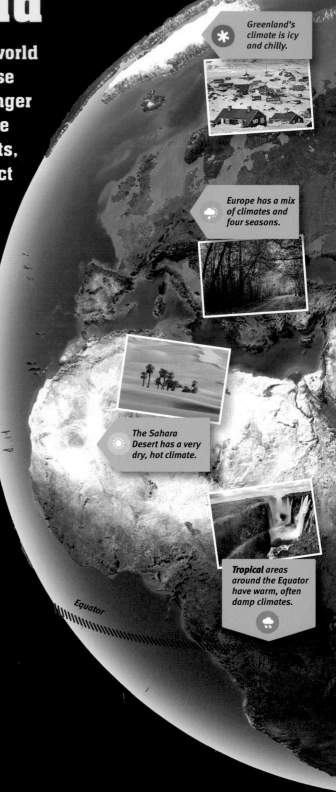

Greenland's climate is icy and chilly.

Europe has a mix of climates and four seasons.

The Sahara Desert has a very dry, hot climate.

Tropical areas around the Equator have warm, often damp climates.

Equator

Other planets can have weather, too. Jupiter, for example, is very stormy.

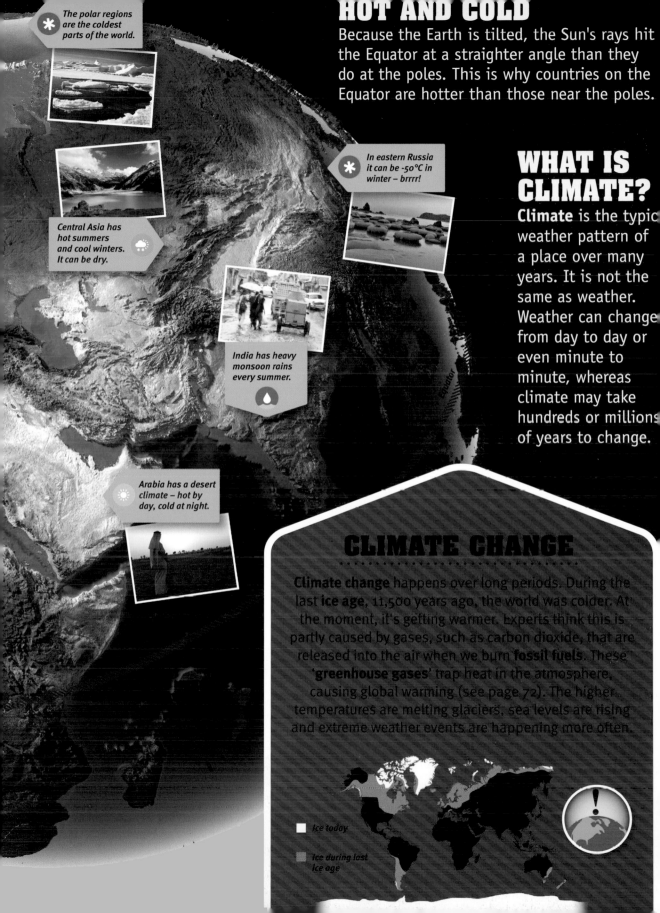

HOT AND COLD

Because the Earth is tilted, the Sun's rays hit the Equator at a straighter angle than they do at the poles. This is why countries on the Equator are hotter than those near the poles.

❋ The polar regions are the coldest parts of the world.

❋ In eastern Russia it can be -50°C in winter – brrrr!

Central Asia has hot summers and cool winters. It can be dry.

India has heavy monsoon rains every summer.

Arabia has a desert climate – hot by day, cold at night.

Equator

WHAT IS CLIMATE?

Climate is the typical weather pattern of a place over many years. It is not the same as weather. Weather can change from day to day or even minute to minute, whereas climate may take hundreds or millions of years to change.

CLIMATE CHANGE

Climate change happens over long periods. During the last **ice age**, 11,500 years ago, the world was colder. At the moment, it's getting warmer. Experts think this is partly caused by gases, such as carbon dioxide, that are released into the air when we burn **fossil fuels**. These '**greenhouse gases**' trap heat in the atmosphere, causing global warming (see page 72). The higher temperatures are melting glaciers, sea levels are rising and extreme weather events are happening more often.

Ice today

Ice during last ice age

The power of the Sun

Most of our weather is caused by something far away from the Earth – the Sun! Besides giving us bright, sunny days, the Sun heats up the Earth and the air around it. The heat makes the air move, causing wind and weather fronts. It also makes water from the oceans, rivers, lakes and plants evaporate into the air, which leads to rain and snow.

▼ Low, thick clouds in the troposphere reflect some of the Sun's light and heat back into space, cooling the Earth's surface.

HEAT FROM THE SUN

As the Sun shines on the Earth, it warms up the Earth's surface. This heat spreads into the troposphere – the layer of air closest to the Earth.

Days and seasons
Find out how the Earth's movements create our days, nights and seasons (see pages 14–15).

Land and sea
Weather near the coast can be very different from the weather far inland (see pages 16–17).

Boiling hot!
Where in the world can you find the hottest weather, and what causes it? (See page 18.)

BOUNCING BACK

How much the Earth reflects heat back into the troposphere depends on a number of things:

IS IT ICY?
Ice caps and glaciers reflect sunshine away.

WHERE IN THE WORLD?
Areas along the Equator get the biggest share of the Sun's energy.

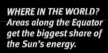

Equator

IS IT CLOUDY? Clouds reflect the Sun's heat and light back into space.

LAND OR SEA? Land heats up in the Sun much faster than water does.

ICY MOUNTAINTOPS

Have you ever wondered why the tops of high mountains are cold and covered with ice and snow? After all, they are nearer the Sun, so why aren't they warmer than the land below?

The reason they are cold is because the temperature in the troposphere decreases the higher up you go. Although sunlight passes through the troposphere from top to bottom, the ground absorbs more of the Sun's heat than the air. The ground then radiates heat back up into the air, which cools as it rises.

As you go higher in the troposphere, the air gets thinner and more spread out. The air pressure is lower, and air at a lower pressure has a lower temperature, making the weather cooler.

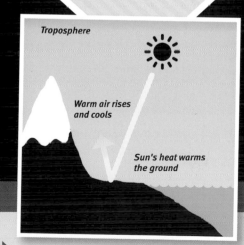

Troposphere

Warm air rises and cools

Sun's heat warms the ground

Heatwaves and heat islands

When extreme heat strikes, it can cause some serious problems (see page 19).

Dry as a bone

The driest weather is found in deserts – but why doesn't it rain there? (See pages 20–21.)

Days and seasons

In most parts of the world, the weather changes according to the seasons. Some places have a warm summer and a cold winter. Other places have a rainy season and a dry season. The weather also changes as day turns to night – it gets colder and darker. Seasons and days happen because of the way the Earth moves around the Sun.

A YEAR ON THE EARTH

The Earth and the other planets orbit (circle around) the Sun. It takes one year for the Earth to make a complete orbit of the Sun and get back to where it started.

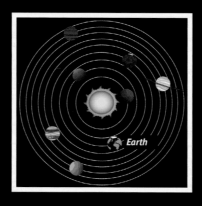

◀ The Earth is the third planet from the Sun.

Earth

SPINNING EARTH

Days happen because the Earth is constantly spinning. It spins right around once every 24 hours. Each day, your home moves into the sunlight, then out of it, so it experiences day and night.

Night   Day

Sunlight

▲ Summer in northern hemisphere. Winter in southern hemisphere.

SUMMER AND WINTER

The Earth is slightly tilted, so for part of the year, the northern **hemisphere** (or half) of the Earth leans towards the Sun. Then, as the Earth moves around, the southern hemisphere leans towards the Sun. It is summer in the hemisphere that is leaning towards the Sun, and winter in the other hemisphere.

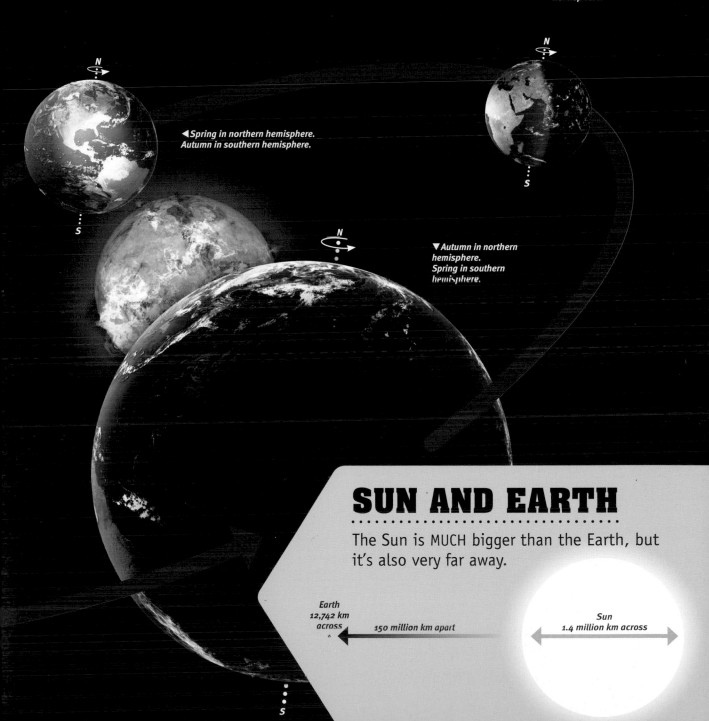

▼ Winter in northern hemisphere. Summer in southern hemisphere.

◄ Spring in northern hemisphere. Autumn in southern hemisphere.

▼ Autumn in northern hemisphere. Spring in southern hemisphere.

SUN AND EARTH

The Sun is MUCH bigger than the Earth, but it's also very far away.

Earth 12,742 km across

150 million km apart

Sun 1.4 million km across

Land and sea

When the Sun shines on land, the land heats up quickly, but it also loses heat quickly. Water, however, heats up slowly. It takes a huge amount of energy from the Sun to warm up the sea. But once it's warm, it cools down slowly. So the sea acts like a big storage tank for the Sun's heat.

▼ Clouds form over this Pacific Ocean island as warm air rises and cools.

▼ Windsurfers take advantage of strong sea breezes.

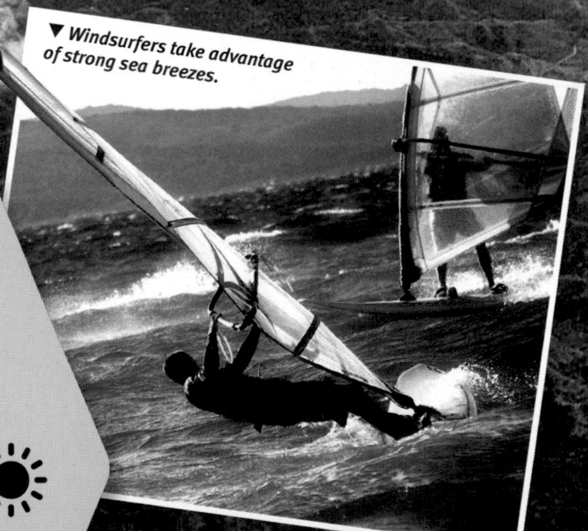

SEA BREEZE

When you're by the sea, you'll often find it's pretty windy. This is because the warm land heats up the air above it, and the air gets lighter and rises. Cool air over the sea then rushes in to take its place, making wind.

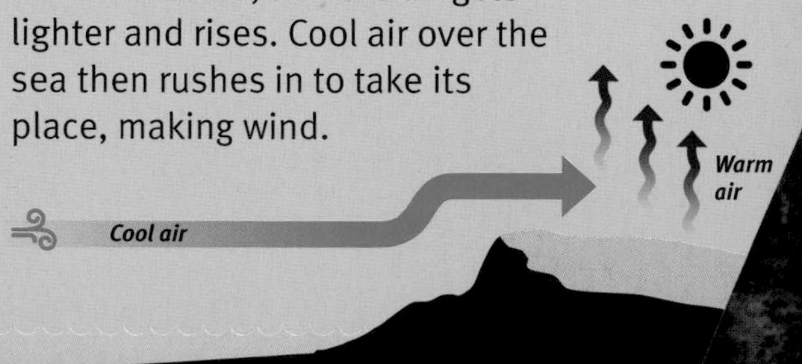

Warm air

Cool air

SIZZLING OR FREEZING INLAND

Far from the sea, temperatures can be more extreme. When it's sunny, the Sun heats up the land fast. The land warms up the air above it, leading to very hot weather. But at night, and in winter, the heat is lost quickly. The temperature drops fast, and winters can be freezing.

HOT AND COLD

- The inland cities of Saskatoon in Canada and Tomsk in Russia have hot summers and very cold winters.

- The United Kingdom (UK) has a more **temperate** climate, with cool winters and warm summers, partly because it is surrounded by sea.

- The climates are different in these places, even though they are all a similar distance from the Equator.

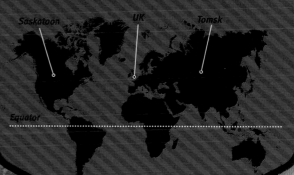

Saskatoon   UK   Tomsk

Equator

COOL AND WARM COASTS

In summer, the sea takes heat from the land, so the land becomes fairly cool. In winter, the sea stores the heat from the Sun that it collected over the summer, and warms the land near the sea. This means that coastal areas tend to have less extreme temperatures than inland areas, which is one reason people love to live near the coast.

▲ People often head to the coast in summer to cool down. This crowded beach is in Dalian City, northern China.

8

Boiling hot!

Most people call hot, sunny weather 'good' weather – but it can get too hot. Sometimes it even feels as if it's boiling hot! The good news is that hot weather is never actually boiling, but how hot does it really get?

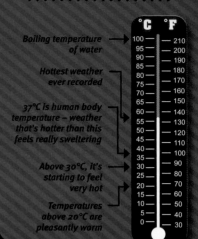

Boiling temperature of water → 100 °C — 210 °F
Hottest weather ever recorded
37°C is human body temperature – weather that's hotter than this feels really sweltering
Above 30°C, it's starting to feel very hot
Temperatures above 20°C are pleasantly warm

HOTTEST WEATHER EVER

The hottest weather in history was recorded on 10 July 1913, in Death Valley, part of the Mojave Desert in California, United States. The temperature was 56.7°C. Water that hot would scald you! Deserts are hot because there are few clouds or plants to block the Sun. The bare sand and rock soak up the Sun's heat, which then heats the air.

▲ Death Valley gets extra hot because it has a deep bowl shape. The air inside the bowl heats up and cannot spread out.

HOTTEST PLACE

Dallol in Ethiopia holds the record for being the hottest inhabited place, with an average daily maximum temperature of 34.4°C. People used to live in a village there, but they've moved away. It must have been too hot!

▼ The volcanic landscape of Dallol is made up of acid ponds and salt desert plains.

Heatwaves and heat islands

In a heatwave, the weather is a lot hotter than usual, and the hot weather lasts for longer than you would expect for the time of year. Heatwaves are caused by a mass of sinking air, which presses down and traps the Sun's heat. This makes the ground and air get hotter and hotter.

▼ Heat islands show up in winter – this city's snow is melting faster than the snow in the surrounding fields.

HEATWAVE HORROR

Heatwaves can be dangerous. Besides being hot, the air is often humid, meaning it is holding a lot of water. We sweat to cool down, but in humid weather it's harder for sweat to evaporate into the air. People easily get too hot and dehydrated (short of water), and this can be deadly.

▼ People in Brussels, Belgium, use water to keep cool during a heatwave in 2015.

HEAT ISLANDS

If a town or city is hotter than the surrounding countryside, it is said to be a 'heat island'. Cities can become heat islands because their bricks, concrete and asphalt heat up in the Sun more than plants. Machines, lights, cars and the heating inside buildings all help to heat cities up even more.

Dry as a bone

Deserts are the driest parts of the world – very little rain falls in a desert. A non-desert area, such as the United Kingdom or New Zealand, receives more than one metre of rainfall in an average year, but a desert receives less than a quarter of that – up to 250 millimetres, and sometimes as little as 10 millimetres.

WHAT MAKES A DESERT?

For rain to fall, there must be clouds. If there are no clouds, there will be no rain and a place will become a desert. Some deserts, such as the Gobi Desert in Asia, are in the middle of large areas of land, far from the seas where most clouds form. Others, such as the Namib Desert in southern Africa, are near the sea, but strong winds blow the damp sea air away, leaving the desert dry.

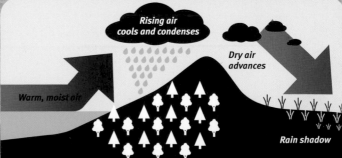

Rising air cools and condenses

Dry air advances

Warm, moist air

Rain shadow

THE RAIN SHADOW EFFECT

Mountains can cause dry desert conditions in the area behind them – their **rain shadow**. As clouds blow towards the mountains, they rise up the slopes, and get colder. This makes the water in them fall as rain. The clouds get used up, so the area beyond the mountains rarely gets rained on.

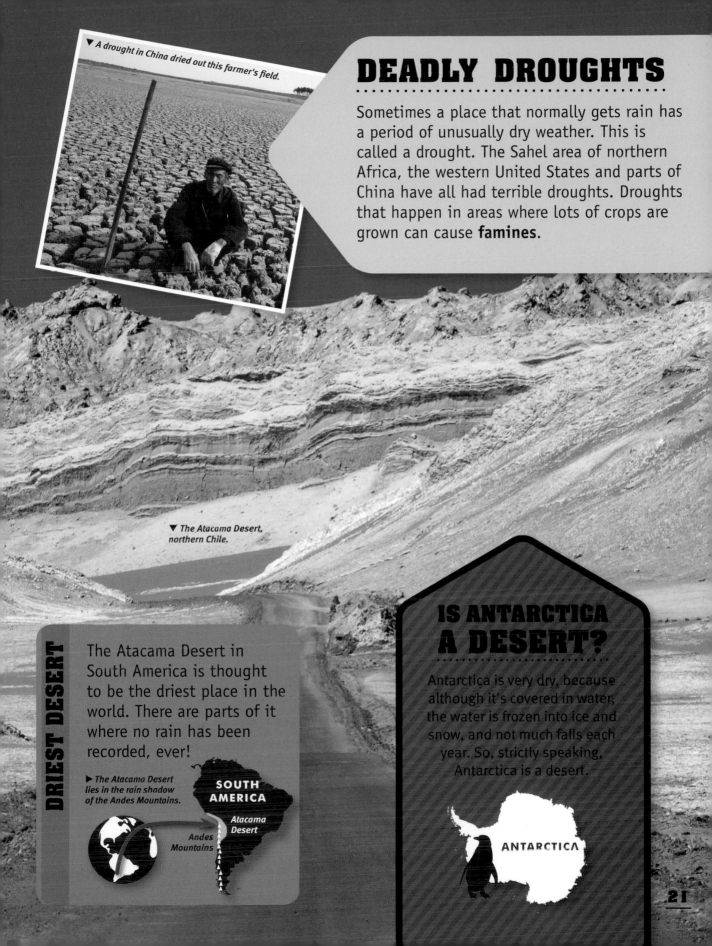

▼ A drought in China dried out this farmer's field.

DEADLY DROUGHTS

Sometimes a place that normally gets rain has a period of unusually dry weather. This is called a drought. The Sahel area of northern Africa, the western United States and parts of China have all had terrible droughts. Droughts that happen in areas where lots of crops are grown can cause **famines**.

▼ The Atacama Desert, northern Chile.

DRIEST DESERT

The Atacama Desert in South America is thought to be the driest place in the world. There are parts of it where no rain has been recorded, ever!

▶ The Atacama Desert lies in the rain shadow of the Andes Mountains.

SOUTH AMERICA

Atacama Desert

Andes Mountains

IS ANTARCTICA A DESERT?

Antarctica is very dry, because although it's covered in water, the water is frozen into ice and snow, and not much falls each year. So, strictly speaking, Antarctica is a desert.

ANTARCTICA

Wild wind

You often don't notice the air that's all around you, especially when you're indoors. But you do notice it when it starts to move. Moving air creates wind. It can blow off your hat or turn your umbrella inside out – and that's just for starters! When wind gets really wild, it can blow down trees, flatten houses and even blow trucks over!

▼ This powerful windstorm on the island of Fiji, in the South Pacific Ocean, is blasting the trees sideways and has shredded the roof of a house.

WIND FACTS

- Wind is the movement of air around the planet.
- The Sun's energy makes the air move by heating it.
- The fastest winds in the world are found inside tornadoes.

Air pressure
Air pressure is the weight of air pushing down on the Earth (see page 24).

Winds of the world
In some parts of the world you can rely on regular wind patterns (see page 25).

Storms
Find out what causes the noisy, windy, wild weather of a storm. (see page 26).

Storm surges
Storm winds can make seawater surge up and flood the land (see page 27).

WHAT MAKES WIND?

Did you know that it's actually heat from the Sun that makes wind? First, sunshine heats up the land. The hot land then heats up the air above it. This warm air spreads out and gets lighter. As it gets lighter, it also rises, allowing colder, heavier air from cooler areas to rush in as wind.

Cooler air moves in to take warm air's place

Wind

Sea

Warm air rises

Land

SUN AND WIND

The Sun heats up some parts of the Earth more than others. Land heats up more than sea, and areas near the Equator heat up more than areas near the poles. This means winds are constantly blowing from one place to another.

CELLS

All over the Earth, warm, rising air creates huge, circulating air systems called **cells**. In one part of a cell, the air rises high into the troposphere. It moves far away, then sinks in another area, moving around in a giant loop.

Cool air

Warm air

Cell

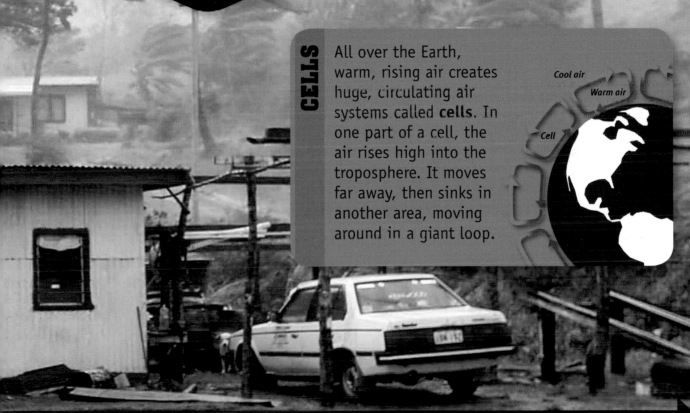

Hurricanes, typhoons and cyclones	Tornadoes	Storm chasing	Waterspouts and dust devils	Dust storms and sandstorms
Hurricanes, typhoons and cyclones are huge storms of wind and rain (see pages 28–29).	These are small, intense whirling windstorms (see page 30).	Some people choose to follow storms! (See page 31.)	More types of tornadoes (see page 32).	Wind and sand can create a scary type of storm (see page 33).

Air pressure

When the atmosphere pushes down on the Earth, it creates air pressure. The air may not seem very heavy, but as the atmosphere is about 100 kilometres deep, there is actually a huge weight of air above us! It presses down and in on us all the time, from all around. The reason you don't feel air pressure squashing you is because you're used to it!

▼ Area of low pressure near Iceland.

MILLIBARS

Weather forecasters measure pressure in **millibars** (mb). The average pressure on the Earth's surface is about 1013 mb.

▼ On weather maps, lines called isobars show pressure. Highs and lows appear as groups of circles.

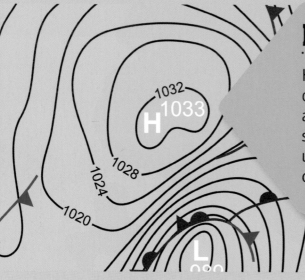

1032
H 1033
1028
1024
1020
L
1980

HIGH PRESSURE

High pressure happens when air is sinking down towards the ground from higher in the atmosphere. The sinking air spreads out slowly, so it is less windy. High pressure usually means calm, settled weather, which can be warm or cool.

LOW PRESSURE

Areas of low pressure, sometimes called 'lows', happen where warmer, lighter air is rising. As the air rises and cools, the water in it forms clouds. The rising air also causes wind, as cooler air rushes in. So low pressure usually means unsettled, cloudy or rainy weather.

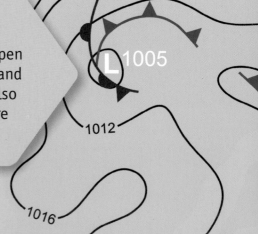

L 1005
1012
1016
1020

L 993
996

Normal air pressure is like a weight of one kilogram on every cm² of your body.

Winds of the world

Local weather may change from day to day, but across the globe winds tend to follow a pattern. The wind that happens most in a particular place is called the **prevailing wind**.

TRADE WINDS

In the days of sailing ships, sailors used the world's prevailing winds to make journeys across oceans. By following particular wind patterns, known as trade winds, they could sail faster. Sometimes, though, they got stuck in less windy areas near the Equator known as the '**doldrums**'.

SIDEWAYS TREE

Sometimes you'll see a tree that has grown leaning over to one side. This is caused by the prevailing wind in that place pushing one side more than the other.

▲ *A windblown tree in Yorkshire, northern England.*

PREVAILING WINDS

The **trade winds**, shown in red, helped sailors to cross from Europe to the Caribbean. The 'westerlies', shown in green, helped them to sail home again! The doldrums (purple band) is an area of light winds. Sailing ships crossing the doldrums were sometimes at a standstill for days.

Storms

What is a storm? It usually means some kind of extreme bad weather. Most storms combine strong winds with other kinds of severe weather, such as heavy rain, thunder and lightning or snow.

Fear of thunder and lightning, in people or animals, is called astraphobia.

WHAT CAUSES A STORM?

Storms form in areas of low pressure, especially if they are surrounded by areas of very high pressure. The low pressure makes air rise, creating strong winds. If there is a lot of water in the air, dark clouds form and produce heavy rain. Storms often occur in summer, when there is lots of heat and **humidity** (damp air).

SWIRLING STORMS

Because of the way the Earth spins, winds swirl in a spiral as they move into a low pressure area. Hurricanes and tornadoes are made of super-fast, spiralling winds. Storms can also move across a region, leaving a trail of destruction behind them.

▶ A rain and lightning storm drenches New Mexico, United States.

TYPES OF STORMS

Snowstorm or blizzard

Electric storm or thunderstorm

Rainstorm

Tornado

Hurricane, typhoon or cyclone

Hailstorm

Ice storm

Storm surges

A storm surge is caused by high winds and low air pressure forming over the sea. High winds push the sea water towards the coast and low pressure causes the sea to rise higher than normal as it does not have as much air pressure pushing down on it. This can cause extensive flooding.

▶ A storm surge swamps part of the town of Whitby in Yorkshire, England.

DEADLY SURGE

One of the deadliest storm surges in history struck Bangladesh and India in 1970, after a huge cyclone formed in the Indian Ocean. The water swamped many of their flat islands and seashore areas, and half a million people died.

ASIA

BANGLADESH

Indian Ocean

RISING WATER

Normally, a slight rise in sea level is not a problem. But if there are also strong winds, a high tide and low-lying land, disaster can follow. Hurricanes often create storm surges. When the extra-high seawater reaches the coast, the water, pushed by the strong winds, rushes ashore.

Storm surge

High tide
Average sea level
Low tide

Hurricanes, typhoons and cyclones

Tropical cyclones have different names depending on where they form. If they start in the Atlantic or eastern Pacific Ocean, they are called hurricanes. If they form in the northwestern Pacific Ocean, they are called typhoons, and if they start in the southwestern Pacific or Indian Ocean they are known as cyclones. They are among the most powerful storms of all.

▼ *The winds of Hurricane Felix were spinning at 265 kilometres per hour as it headed west across the Caribbean Sea.*

Hurricane winds can reach speeds of more than 300 kilometres per hour.

▲ *Hurricane Fran, which formed in the Atlantic Ocean, is seen here from above, about to make landfall in Florida, United States.*

HOW HURRICANES WORK

Hurricanes form over warm tropical oceans, and can grow to be 900 kilometres across in just a few days. The heat from the Sun warms the water and makes it evaporate into the air. As the moist air heats up and rises, the water in the air forms a mass of heavy rainclouds. Cooler air then rushes in to replace the rising air, swirling in a spiral because of the way the Earth rotates.

▶ *Weather forecasters sometimes give large tropical cyclones their own names. This satellite image shows Hurricane Felix – a major 2007 hurricane – from above. The gap in the middle is the eye of the hurricane.*

EYE OF THE HURRICANE

In a hurricane, air is mostly rising, but right in the middle the air sinks down, creating a cloud-free spot called the 'eye' of the storm. The bank of clouds around the eye, called the 'eyewall', is the windiest, wettest part of the storm. The weather in the eye itself is much calmer.

▼ *A typical hurricane can be 450 kilometres across.*

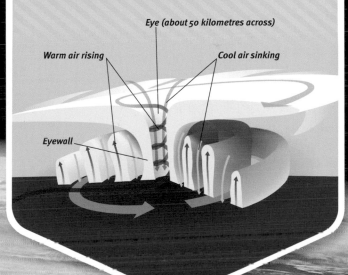

Eye (about 50 kilometres across)

Warm air rising

Cool air sinking

Eyewall

MORE ON THE WAY...

For a hurricane to form, the surface of the sea needs to be about 26°C or above. At the moment, the Earth's climate is warming up (see pages 72–73). This means seas will reach the trigger temperature more often, so we will probably see more hurricanes.

STORM DAMAGE

Hurricane Sandy was one of the most devastating hurricanes of recent years, tearing through the Caribbean and North America in October of 2012. Its strong winds and heavy rain caused floods, cut off power and destroyed homes from Jamaica all the way to Ontario, Canada.

▲ ▶ *These houses were blown off their foundations by Hurricane Sandy.*

17 ▶ **Tornadoes**

Tornadoes are the scariest, wildest windstorms in the world. They may not be the biggest storms, but they have the most powerful winds. A tornado's energy is concentrated in a small area. Its spiralling wind spins tightly down to the ground in a funnel shape, and destroys anything in its path.

BORN IN A STORM

Tornadoes usually form as part of a thunderstorm. When a mass of cold, dry air meets warm, damp air, the warmer air rises and forms thunderclouds. Sometimes, when the cold air meets the warm air, they start to spin in a column. Rain and hail then push the spinning air down towards the ground.

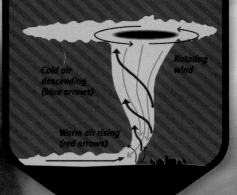

Cold air descending (blue arrows)

Rotating wind

Warm air rising (red arrows)

◀ This tornado in Kansas, United States, has whipped up the dusty earth into its funnel.

UP IN THE AIR

Tornado winds are so powerful that they can lift roofs, cars, trucks or sheds off the ground and fling them around. People have even been carried through the air. In 1955, this happened to a nine-year-old girl riding a pony! They both survived.

Storm chasing

The most sensible thing to do if you see a tornado coming is to run away, or hide in an underground storm shelter. But some people actually chase tornadoes! They follow them to take photos or videos, or study the tornadoes to find out more about them.

IT'S GOING THAT WAY!

Storm chasers often report their tornado sightings to weather forecasters. This helps the forecasters to predict where the tornado will go next.

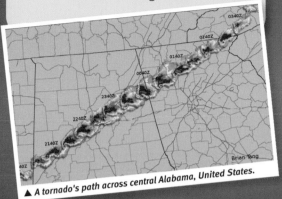

▲ A tornado's path across central Alabama, United States.

READY TO GO...

Storm chasers focus on areas that get a lot of tornadoes, such as the central part of the United States, known as Tornado Alley. When a tornado is spotted, they follow it by car, or sometimes by plane or helicopter. They have to be careful not to get too close, though!

TORNADO NUMBERS

- The fastest tornado winds ever reached 512 kilometres per hour.

- Tornadoes range from about 100 metres to 4 kilometres wide.

- A tornado can travel a distance of up to 480 kilometres.

◄ Storm chasers gather to film a tornado in South Dakota, United States.

Waterspouts and dust devils

Waterspouts and dust devils are mini-tornadoes that can form over water or over dry, hot, dusty places, such as deserts. They are smaller and weaker than normal tornadoes, and usually not as dangerous.

Waterspouts sometimes suck up sea creatures from the water into the sky. This could be an explanation for the weird 'animal rain' that can happen (see page 62).

▲ A dust devil often looks like a cloud of smoke moving across the desert.

WATERSPOUTS

Waterspouts appear over water, but they aren't actually made of solid water – they are mostly made of cloud or mist. A waterspout can grow upwards from the water as warm air rises, or it can reach down from a cloud, like a normal tornado.

DUST DEVILS

A dust devil forms when hot air just above the ground starts to move upwards. As it meets the cooler air above it, it begins to twist into a spiral. The moving air sucks up dust or sand, making the dust devil easy to see. In some countries, dust devils were traditionally seen as desert spirits or ghosts.

▲ A waterspout looks like a writhing, watery snake as it stretches between the sea and the clouds.

Du t storms a nd sandstorms

One of the scariest weather sights you can see is a huge, dark wall of sand or dust rolling towards you. These storms happen when strong winds pick up lots of desert sand or dusty, dried-out soil. They are common in dry areas, such as northern Africa and Arabia.

DANGEROUS DUST!

A big sandstorm or dust storm can be a horrible experience. The flying particles get in your eyes and mouth, and down your throat. The storm can make it impossible to see, causing car accidents. Sandstorms can also drop huge heaps or drifts of sand that can bury cars, houses and crops.

▼ A dust storm billows across the western desert of Iraq. It was estimated to be between 1200 to 1500 metres tall.

Camels can close their nostrils tight to help them survive sandstorms.

THE DUST BOWL

DUST BOWL

Denver .

. Topeka

Santa Fe .

. Oklahoma City

Austin
.

In the United States in the 1930s, a serious drought made a large area of the country horribly dusty and dry. It became known as the Dust Bowl. Giant dust storms in the area caused people serious illnesses by making it hard for them to breathe.

World of water

When you think of weather, you often think of water. Clouds, rain, snow, hail, sleet, mist and fog – they're all made of water, floating around in the atmosphere... or falling on your head! When water comes out of the air and falls to the ground in any form, it's called **precipitation**.

HOW MUCH WATER?

At any one time, the atmosphere contains about 13,000 cubic kilometres of water. That's about as much water as there is in a big lake, such as Lake Superior in North America. If all this water fell out of the sky at once, it would cover the world in a layer of water about 2.5 centimetres deep.

WATER IN THE AIR

The atmosphere always contains some water – but how does the water get into the air?

 The Sun's heat makes water evaporate into the air from oceans, seas, lakes and rivers.

 Water also evaporates from damp land and soil.

 Snow and ice can evaporate directly into gas and float off into the air.

 Plants release water into the air from their leaves.

▶ Heavy downpours, such as this one in Thailand, are common in tropical countries.

Clouds
Clouds are made of water droplets in the air (see page 36).

Strange clouds
Some clouds look extremely weird (see page 37).

What is rain?
Raindrops fall when a cloud cools (see pages 38–39).

Rainstorms
A burst of heavy rain can cause floods (see page 40).

How wet does it get?
Find out about the world's wettest places (see page 41).

THE WATER CYCLE

Water constantly moves around the atmosphere. This is called the water cycle. On average, water stays in the air for about nine days before falling back to the Earth's surface.

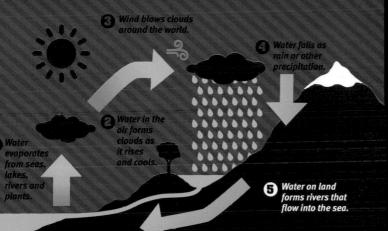

3 Wind blows clouds around the world.

4 Water falls as rain or other precipitation.

2 Water in the air forms clouds as it rises and cools.

1 Water evaporates from seas, lakes, rivers and plants.

5 Water on land forms rivers that flow into the sea.

MISTY BREATH

When people and animals breathe out, they breathe water into the air. That's why when you go out on a very cold day, you can see your breath as a 'cloud'. The cold air makes the water vapour, or gas, from your body condense into droplets that are big enough to see.

▲ When it's very cold, your breath makes a mini-cloud.

WATER FACTS

● The atmosphere always contains some water.

● Precipitation is water falling from the atmosphere as different forms of weather.

● Water constantly moves between the atmosphere and the Earth's surface in a process called the water cycle.

Floods
Too much rain can cause floods (see pages 42–43).

Thunder and lightning
These are born inside storm clouds (see pages 44–45).

Fog, mist and smog
Find out what it's like to be inside a cloud (see page 46).

Rainbows
Find out how rainbows are made (see page 47).

Wind and waves
Sea waves can cause floods (see page 48).

Seiches
The sloshing of water in a lake (see page 49).

Clouds

Clouds form when water vapour changes from a gas into tiny water droplets. This happens when the air gets cooler. In the troposphere – the part of the atmosphere closest to the ground – the air gets cooler the higher up you go, so clouds usually form high in the sky.

WHITE AND FLUFFY

If the water droplets in a cloud are very small and tightly packed, they reflect more light, and the cloud looks white. Sometimes the droplets freeze into tiny white ice crystals.

◀ *Fluffy white clouds like these are cumulus clouds.*

CLOUD-SPOTTING

▲ *Altocumulus* ▲ *Altostratus* ▲ *Cirrocumulus* ▲ *Cirrus*

▲ *Cumulonimbus* ▲ *Cumulus* ▲ *Stratocumulus* ▲ *Stratus*

Clouds come in various shapes and types, and each type has its own name. How many of these have you seen?

DARK AND STORMY

When it's about to rain, clouds can look grey. This is because the water in the clouds has formed larger droplets that reflect less light, so the cloud looks grey. The undersides of clouds can also look dark, as sunlight cannot easily shine through them.

Strange clouds

BANNER CLOUD

This is a banner cloud, which clings to one side of a mountain. Banner clouds form as damp air is pushed high up a mountainside by the wind.

The clouds on the opposite page are common types that we see all the time. But once in a while, very odd-looking clouds can form!

LENTICULAR CLOUDS

Lenticular clouds are called lenticular because they are shaped like lenses. They usually form over the tops of high mountains as damp air piles up in one place. Some are so round that they look similar to alien spaceships or UFOs.

▲ *At first glance this lenticular cloud really does look like a flying saucer!*

MAMMATUS CLOUDS

A mammatus cloud has strange, sack-like shapes hanging down from its base. Weather scientists aren't sure exactly how these shapes form, but they think it's something to do with warm and cool air swirling around in patterns under the cloud.

◄ *This huge mass of odd-looking mammatus clouds was caught on camera in Germany.*

Some UFO sightings may actually have been lenticular clouds!

What is rain?

We might moan when a rainy day ruins our plans, but rain is one of the most important types of weather there is. Thanks to rain, crops and other plants can grow, and people and animals have water to drink. Without rain, our world would be very different.

WATER DROPLETS

Warm air can hold much more water vapour than cold air. In cold air, the water vapour condenses and turns into liquid droplets. At a certain point, these drops become so big and heavy that the air can no longer hold them up. Gravity pulls them to the ground in the form of rain.

▲ Medium to heavy raindrops such as these measure about 0.5 centimetres across. Smaller drops are called drizzle.

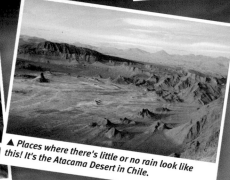

▲ Places where there's little or no rain look like this! It's the Atacama Desert in Chile.

▲ Streams, rivers and waterfalls, such as this one in Thailand, are only there because rain falls on the land.

▶ A spectacular cloudburst in July 2015 dropped heavy rain and hail on to the streets of Las Vegas, United States.

A typical raindrop lands on you at a speed of about 30 kilometres per hour.

HOW RAIN FORMS

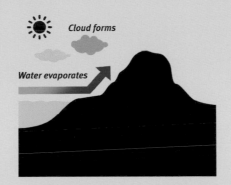

Cloud forms

Water evaporates

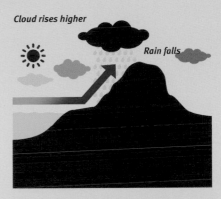

Cloud rises higher

Rain falls

1 The Sun heats the land and sea, making water evaporate into the air. As the water vapour rises and cools, it forms water droplets, which form clouds.

2 As the clouds rise higher, they get even colder, and the water in them turns into heavy raindrops. These fall as rain.

MEASURING RAIN

Weather scientists record rainfall using an instrument called a rain gauge. This measures the amount of rain that falls over a certain period of time. Rain falls into the top of the gauge and collects at the bottom, where it can be measured against a scale bar.

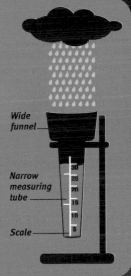

Wide funnel

Narrow measuring tube

Scale

30
25
20
15
10
5

Rainstorms

A rainstorm is a period of extra-heavy rain. Rainstorms are more common in the summer, when hot weather makes more water evaporate from the land and seas. The water droplets in the air then form big rainclouds, which release rain that is heavier than normal.

A cloudburst is a very fast, heavy but short rainstorm.

SUDDEN DOWNPOUR

In a big rainstorm, the rain tends to be heavy and fast. The drops are big and close together, so a lot of water falls in a short space of time. If the rain falls onto soil, grass or trees on fairly flat land, it can soak into the ground, but when heavy rain falls in hilly areas, it can end up rushing down into valleys or lower areas, causing floods.

RAIN DISASTERS

Heavy rain can cause serious problems for people:

- 🌧 It can damage crops by flattening or swamping them.

- 🌧 It can soak into soil on steep slopes and cause landslides or cliff-collapses.

- 🌧 It can make rivers and lakes overflow.

▼ Heavy rain soaking into soil can cause dangerous landslides, such as this one in Japan.

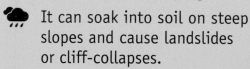
▲ A deep, low cloud such as this can release a sudden rainstorm.

How wet does it get?

The wettest parts of the world are mainly in the tropics – the areas closest to the Equator. This is where the weather is warmest, and where most water evaporates into the atmosphere. Super-soggy spots include Hawaii, West Africa, northern India and Colombia.

▼ No one's going to be travelling on this Indian railway line, which has been damaged by a flood.

RAINDROP RECORD

The biggest-ever raindrops were recorded over Brazil and the Pacific Ocean. They were one centimetre across – almost as big as a marble.

Typical raindrop 2 millimetres

Record-breaking raindrop 10 millimetres

WETTEST PLACE TO LIVE

Several places claim to be the rainiest in the world, but most experts agree that the village of Mawsynram in India holds the record. It has an average rainfall of 11,872 millimetres a year (almost 12 metres) – enough rain to cover a four-storey building! In 1985, it received a record-breaking 26 metres of rain.

Enough water falls on the world each year to fill 500 trillion swimming pools!

Floods

In a flood, water flows over land that is normally dry. That can be good news – some rivers flood every year, watering the fields around them. But if a flood happens where people live, it can be devastating. Floods have caused some of the worst natural disasters in history.

As sea levels rise, flooding along the coast will become more common.

GETTING WETTER!

As the world gets warmer (see page 72), experts think there will be more floods. Why?

• Hotter temperatures mean more water evaporating into the air – and more rain.

• Ice at the poles is melting into the sea, making sea levels rise. So it's easier for storm surges, big waves and high tides to flow over the tops of sea walls and onto the land.

FLOOD CAUSES

Floods happen for two main reasons:

❶ Rain may drench the land and fill up rivers, causing them to overflow their banks.

❷ Sea storms and rising sea levels can flood the land with seawater.

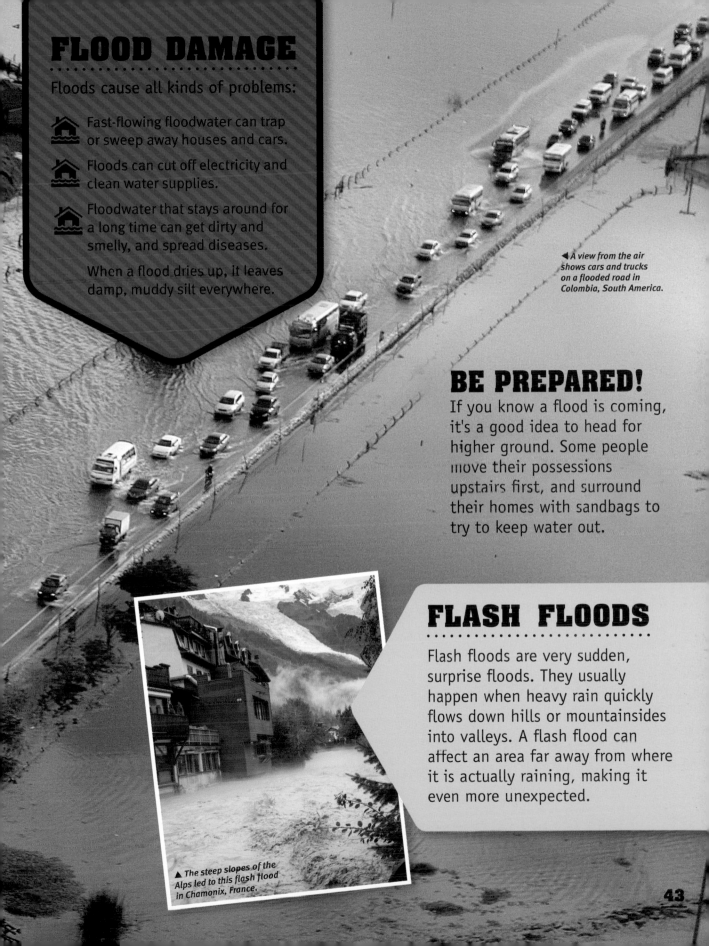

FLOOD DAMAGE

Floods cause all kinds of problems:

- Fast-flowing floodwater can trap or sweep away houses and cars.
- Floods can cut off electricity and clean water supplies.
- Floodwater that stays around for a long time can get dirty and smelly, and spread diseases.

When a flood dries up, it leaves damp, muddy silt everywhere.

◀ A view from the air shows cars and trucks on a flooded road in Colombia, South America.

BE PREPARED!

If you know a flood is coming, it's a good idea to head for higher ground. Some people move their possessions upstairs first, and surround their homes with sandbags to try to keep water out.

FLASH FLOODS

Flash floods are very sudden, surprise floods. They usually happen when heavy rain quickly flows down hills or mountainsides into valleys. A flash flood can affect an area far away from where it is actually raining, making it even more unexpected.

▲ The steep slopes of the Alps led to this flash flood in Chamonix, France.

43

Thunder and lightning

Thunderstorms, or electric storms, happen when lots of warm, wet air rises quickly into the sky. As the warm air cools, it piles up into tall thunderclouds that can produce lightning, heavy rain, hail or snow.

HOW LIGHTNING HAPPENS

Thunderclouds reach high into the atmosphere, where it is so cold that the water droplets in the cloud freeze into ice crystals and small hailstones. These bump and rub against each other, causing static electricity to build up – just as it does when you rub a balloon against your jumper. The electrical energy in the thundercloud is released in the form of giant sparks, called lightning.

LIGHTNING RODS

Most tall buildings have a metal lightning rod or conductor attached to the roof. A wire from the rod runs down the side of the building and into the ground. If lightning strikes the rod, the electric charge is carried safely away from the building, down the wire and into the earth.

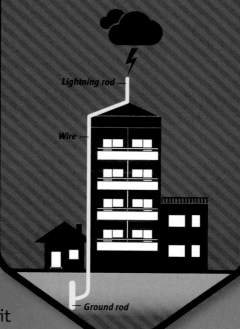

Lightning rod

Wire

Ground rod

FORKED AND SHEET

Lightning that jumps between a cloud and the ground is called forked lightning. If it jumps from one part of a cloud to another, it's called sheet lightning.

MORE LIGHTNING

Lightning is constantly striking the Earth somewhere. Strikes happen about 50 times a second! Global warming is increasing this rate, as more warm air produces more thunderstorms.

WHAT IS THUNDER?

Thunder is the sound of lightning! A lightning flash heats up the air around it, making it explode. This creates a shock wave that we hear as a loud crash or rumble. Light travels much faster than sound, so we always see the lightning flash before we hear the thunder.

◄ *This powerful lightning storm is making multiple strikes on a city in Lebanon.*

LIGHTNING STRIKES

A lightning spark takes the shortest path it can between the cloud and the ground, so it usually strikes tall things. If you ever get caught in a thunderstorm, remember:

 Never shelter under a tree.

 Stay away from hilltops.

 Do not wave an umbrella, golf club or other metal object in the air.

Fog, mist and smog

▼ San Francisco in the United States is famous for its coastal sea fogs.

Clouds are normally found high in the sky, but not always! When a cloud forms close to the ground, it's called fog or mist.

FOG OR MIST?

Just like a cloud, fog is made of water droplets floating in the air. The droplets form when damp air gets very cold, and the water vapour in the air condenses into tiny drops of liquid. Fog and mist are the same thing, but fog is thicker. If you can see for at least one kilometre (1000 metres), you are in mist. If you can't see that far, you are in fog.

KILLER SMOG

Fog often forms in cities, because water droplets condense easily around tiny specks of dust or smoke in the air. A mixture of pollution and fog is called **smog**. It can cause breathing problems and make people ill.

WHERE DOES FOG FORM?

You may see fog in any of these places:

Close to the ground on a winter morning, after the very cold ground has cooled the air.

In valleys, where cold air sinks and collects at the bottom.

At sea, when the wind blows damp air over cold seawater.

Very thick fog, with visibility below 100 metres, can cause road accidents.

Rainbows

There are few weather sights more beautiful than a brilliant rainbow arching across the sky. Long ago, people thought rainbows must be magical, because they were so perfectly shaped and shone with such strong colours.

RAINBOWS EVERYWHERE

You don't only see rainbows in rain. You can sometimes see them in fog, misty clouds or the spray from a waterfall. You can even make your own rainbow by standing with your back to the Sun and spraying a fine mist with a garden hose.

▲ We see a whole rainbow because we are looking at many raindrops, all bending and separating the Sun's light.

FINDING RAINBOWS

To see a rainbow, you must have the Sun behind you and the raindrops in front of you.

Sunlight

Sun

Raindrop

Rainbow

MOONBOW

Very bright moonlight at night sometimes creates a rainbow called a 'moonbow'.

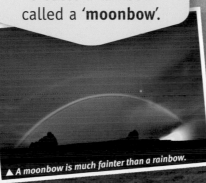

▲ A moonbow is much fainter than a rainbow.

WHAT MAKES A RAINBOW?

For a rainbow to happen, you need two things – sunlight and raindrops. Sunlight is 'white' light, which is made up of many colours. When a ray of white light shines into a raindrop, the ray bends and reflects off the back of the raindrop, and the colours separate and spread out to form a rainbow.

Wind and waves

Boats make waves as they push through water, and people make waves when they jump in. However, most of the waves that we see are made by wind.

WHERE DO WAVES COME FROM?

Out at sea, wind blows over the surface of the water, pushing and disturbing it so that it ripples and forms waves. The stronger the wind, and the longer it blows, the bigger the waves will be. Waves also grow bigger when the wind blows them over a long distance.

▼ A surfer zooms along the steep front of a wave as it rolls forward and breaks!

WHY WAVES BREAK

At sea, waves ripple forward through the water, but rarely break. As they approach the shore, they move into shallower water. As the bottom part of the wave drags over the seabed, the top part piles up, tips over and breaks.

Wave direction

Wave breaking

As waves reach the shore, they tower up...

... and tip over, or break.

Seabed

▲ Powerful storm waves batter a coastal railway in southern England.

DANGEROUS WAVES

In a storm, especially when there's a storm surge (see page 27), big waves can pour over sea walls and smash up railways, roads and buildings. They may even wash away people who get too close.

The biggest waves ever surfed were as tall as a 12-storey building.

48

Seiches

A seiche is a rare event. It's the sloshing back and forth of water in a lake or an enclosed bay – like water in a bath when you stir it with your hand. A severe seiche can cause water to flood onto the shore and wash people away.

▼ *A combination of seiches, wind and high tides caused this flood in Venice, Italy.*

WHAT MAKES THEM

The main causes of seiches are:

Strong storm winds

High air pressure

Volcanic eruptions

Earthquakes

Landslides into water

SEICHE DISASTER

A deadly seiche struck Lake Michigan in the United States in 1954. As the water level rose near the city of Chicago, it washed away people who were fishing on a pier, drowning eight of them.

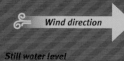

Wind direction

High water due to wind setup

Still water level

Wind setup is a local rise in water level caused by wind.

SLOSHING WATER

Lake water sloshes to and fro all the time, but usually the change in water level is not noticeable. With a seiche, strong storm winds, high air pressure, or movements from a volcano, earthquake or landslide can make the water move, so that it sinks down in one area, and rises up in another. The water then sloshes back the other way.

Freezing cold

◀ Icicles, such as these ones in Toronto, Canada, form when water freezes as it drips.

When freezing cold temperatures and water come together, they create snow and ice. Freezing weather is common in places that have cold winters, such as Canada, Russia and Austria. You also get snow and ice at the tops of mountains, and at the Earth's poles – the coldest places in the world.

▼ If it's cold enough, puddles, ponds and lakes can freeze over.

TAKE CARE!

Ice and snow can be fun, but people need to be careful not to slip and slide or get stuck in the snow – especially when driving. Ice is slippery because it's very smooth, hard and wet, so it's hard for shoes and tyres to get a grip.

▲ Severe winter weather often causes traffic jams and hold-ups. These drivers have come to a standstill.

Snowstorms and blizzards
When you get a storm and snow together, the weather can be very extreme (see page 52).

Avalanches
When snow piles up on a slope, it can cause a dangerous avalanche (see page 53).

Hail
Find out what makes balls of solid ice shower down from the sky (see pages 54–55).

TYPES OF FROZEN WEATHER

1. SNOW – fluffy flakes made up of delicate ice crystals
2. SLEET – snow that has started to melt as it falls
3. HAILSTONES – hard, solid balls of ice
4. GRAUPEL – softer ice balls, a cross between hail and snow
5. FROST – an icy coating that forms when water from the air freezes onto surfaces
6. FREEZING RAIN – rain that freezes onto cold surfaces
7. GLAZE – A build-up of clear ice on trees and wires, made by freezing rain

▼ Snow can pile up into deep snowdrifts when it is blown by the wind.

ICE CRYSTALS

Snow and ice are made of frozen water. Light, fluffy snowflakes form when tiny water droplets in clouds freeze into small ice crystals that gradually join together. Harder hailstones form in storm clouds when large water droplets are carried high into the sky and freeze solid into blocks of ice. Water that's already on the ground can also freeze, making pavements slippery and puddles ice over.

▲ Seen through a microscope, each snowflake has its own intricate shape.

FLUFFY FLAKES

Snowflakes form slowly as ice crystals join together. They start as a hexagon (six-sided) shape, and then grow six branches from the corners of the hexagon. Each fluffy 'flake' contains many of these six-sided shapes.

Ice storms
Strangely quiet and still, ice storms are rare and fascinating (see pages 56–57).

Frost
How does frost manage to cover everything in a crunchy, feathery coating? (See page 58.)

How cold does it get?
Find out about the coldest places you can go, and what it's like there (see page 59).

Snowstorm— and blizzards

In a snowstorm, a great deal of snow falls and builds up on the ground. If strong winds blow the snow in all directions as it falls, the snowstorm is called a blizzard, or 'whiteout'. It can be almost impossible to see where you're going during a blizzard.

▶ After a snowstorm hit Boston, United States, in January 2015, the snow was so deep you could snowboard down the street!

SNOW DANGERS

Heavy snow is great fun for sledging, snowballing and building snowmen, but it can cause people lots of problems:

❄ Deep snow makes it hard for cars, buses and trains to get around.

❄ Big snowdrifts can blow up against houses and trap people inside.

❄ The weight of snow can make gutters and roofs collapse, and bring down tree branches.

WATCH OUT FOR WINDCHILL!

Wind can make the temperature feel much colder than it actually is. This is called the 'windchill factor'. Just as a breeze can cool you down on a hot day, when it's cold, wind can make you feel even colder. In a blizzard, strong winds can chill you to the bone!

LOST IN THE SNOW

In a severe blizzard, the whiteout can be so bad that you can't see what's right in front of your face. People have been known to get lost in blizzards even when they were very close to houses and safety.

Avalanches

An avalanche happens when a mass of snow piles up on a slope and becomes so heavy that it suddenly slips downhill. Avalanches can be quite small, but in high mountain ranges, such as the Alps in Europe and the Himalayas in Asia, they are often huge and deadly dangerous.

BURIED BY SNOW

Avalanches are a risk for skiers and mountain hikers. The heavy, fast-moving snow can crush and injure anyone it lands on, or bury people so that they can't breathe. Some avalanches have even buried whole houses and villages.

▼ A powerful avalanche crashes down Pumori in the Himalayas.

SURVIVE AN AVALANCHE

If you ever get caught in an avalanche, here's what you should do:

- Run sideways to get out of the avalanche's way.
- Drop heavy bags – they will make you sink.
- Try to 'swim' with your arms to stay on top of the moving snow.
- If you get buried in snow, hold your arms in front of your face.
- Dig a hole in front of your face to help you breathe while you wait for rescuers to find you.

ROOF AVALANCHE

A mini-avalanche can happen when snow suddenly slides off a roof and lands in a heap. This can happen after a heavy snowfall, or when snow begins to melt.

36 ▶ Hail

You may dash from a rainstorm because you don't want to get wet, but when it starts to hail... you'll want to run for cover! Rock-solid balls of ice falling on your head can really hurt, even when they are normal, pea-sized hailstones – but they can be much bigger!

HOW HAIL HAPPENS

Hail only forms in thunderclouds. The clouds are very tall, and contain fast-moving air currents that blow upwards and downwards. Sometimes water droplets from low in the cloud get blown up to the top, where it's freezing cold, and turn into balls of ice. As they move around in the cloud, more layers of ice build up around them. When they are too heavy to stay up, they fall as hail.

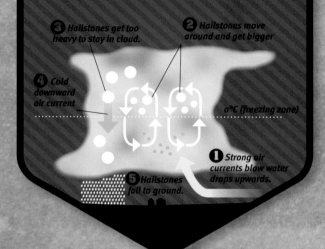

❸ Hailstones get too heavy to stay in cloud.

❷ Hailstones move around and get bigger

❹ Cold downward air current

0°C (freezing zone)

❶ Strong air currents blow water drops upwards.

❺ Hailstones fall to ground.

HALF A HAILSTONE

If you cut a large hailstone in half, you'll see that it is made up of layers of ice – a bit like the growth rings in a slice of tree trunk.

▼ A violent hailstorm approaching can be a scary sight!

HAIL SWATHS

Hailstorms are usually sudden and heavy, and only last for a few minutes. During this time they often move across the land, leaving a long, narrow trail of hail, called a hail swath. As well as leaving piles of hailstones on the ground, a hailstorm can dent cars and smash windows, damage roofs, flatten crops and cut off power supplies.

▲ A ten minute hailstorm in Buenos Aires, Argentina, in 2013, left 5000 cars damaged by hailstones the size of golf balls!

◀ Caught in a sudden hailstorm, these people are running to safety – but their umbrella might not survive!

RECORD HAILSTONES

Hailstones are normally the size of a pea, but they can be much bigger! The biggest hailstones are 'aggregate' hailstones, meaning they are made up of lots of smaller hailstones clumped together. The largest aggregate hailstone ever measured fell in Vivian, South Dakota, United States, in 2010. At 20 centimetres across, it was as big as a melon!

Football

Melon

Golf ball

Pea

Ice storms

Imagine opening your front door and looking out to see everything around you covered in thick, gleaming ice! This is what happens in an ice storm, which is caused by freezing rain.

▼ This amazing ice glaze in Switzerland formed when spray blowing from Lake Geneva fell onto freezing cold objects.

QUIET STORM

Most storms are wild, windy and noisy, but not an ice storm! The rain can fall quietly and freeze silently, so a person may not even know the storm has happened until they go outside. There may just be a sudden cracking sound as heavy ice snaps branches off trees.

ICE GLAZE

The build-up of ice caused by freezing rain is called glaze. In ice storms, glaze can be up to 20 centimetres thick! Although it's beautiful, it's also dangerous because it's so heavy. A layer just two centimetres thick can bring down tree branches and power cables, while glaze on a road surface (black ice) is hard to see and is too slippery to drive on.

WHAT MAKES AN ICE STORM?

As rain lands on icy-cold ground, or on cold trees, buildings, fences and houses, it freezes solid, building up a layer of ice all over them.

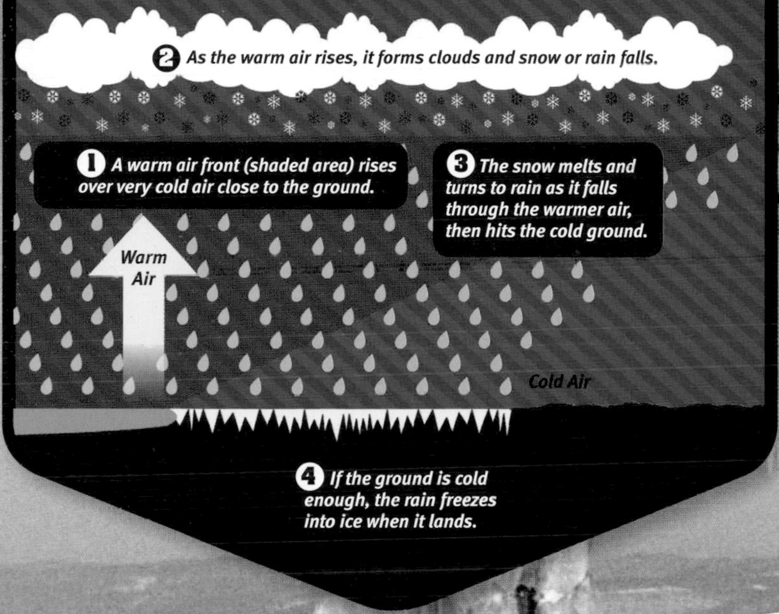

2 As the warm air rises, it forms clouds and snow or rain falls.

1 A warm air front (shaded area) rises over very cold air close to the ground.

Warm Air

3 The snow melts and turns to rain as it falls through the warmer air, then hits the cold ground.

Cold Air

4 If the ground is cold enough, the rain freezes into ice when it lands.

▼ Havoc wreaked by an ice storm in Oklahoma, United States.

CUT OFF!

In a severe ice storm, fallen power lines cut off electricity supplies, and fallen trees and black ice make roads impassable. People can end up trapped in their homes without heating, and it can be hard for rescuers to reach them.

Frost

Frost is a coating of ice that appears on the ground, on grass, on trees and on smooth surfaces such as windows. It's made when water vapour in the air freezes.

▲ Frost can create a beautiful, sparkling coating on fruits and leaves.

FROZEN DEW

Dew is water that condenses from the air onto outdoor surfaces when the temperature drops overnight. In very cold weather, dew forms as ice, and we call it frost. The ice crystals in frost can form delicate, hair-like shapes that make frost appear spiky, fluffy or even furry.

▶ Hoar frost is white, flaky frost that forms on cold objects overnight.

FOLKLORE
According to some fairy tales, frost is left behind by a mischievous sprite. In some countries the sprite is called Jack Frost, and in others Mother Frost or Grandfather Frost.

▲ This frost has grown into detailed feather-like shapes.

WINDOW FROST

In freezing weather, frost can form on the inside of an ice-cold window. When moisture in the air touches the window, it freezes into ice crystals. As the crystals spread across the glass, they can form patterns that look like feathers, trees or ferns.

COLDEST WEATHER EVER

The coldest weather ever recorded was -89.2°C, measured at Vostok research station in Antarctica, in 1983. That's almost as far below zero as boiling is above zero! (It can get even colder high up in the Earth's atmosphere, but weather temperatures are recorded at ground level.)

How cold does it get?

Water freezes at 0°C, so when the temperature drops this low, we may get snow or ice, and it feels cold outside. But it can get a lot colder than 0°C!

ICE AGES

The Earth's climate warms up and cools down over long periods of time. There have been several ice ages, when it was much colder than it is now. About 20,000 years ago, it was so cold that huge glaciers covered the land around the North Pole, reaching as far south as today's London and New York.

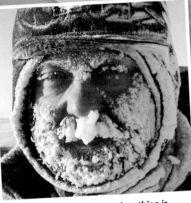

▲ In very low temperatures, breathing is painful and frost can form on your face! Noses, fingers and toes sometimes freeze and begin to die – a condition known as **frostbite**.

▼Snow, ice and huge glaciers such as this one still cover most of Greenland.

▲ The South Pole is the world's most southerly point. A ceremonial pole, shown here, stands near the geograpical South Pole.

▲ This is the front edge of the glacier. It creeps forward as the ice slowly flows downhill.

COLDEST PLACE

Antarctica, the land mass around the South Pole, is the world's coldest place. At the South Pole, the average temperature through the year is about -49°C, which is much colder than your kitchen freezer!

Weird weather

Most weather – even something as striking as a rainbow – is quite familiar to us. But once in a while, weather gets very weird indeed! It can put on an amazing display of strange lights, shower us with animals, or even make you see something that isn't there...

SEEING THINGS!

A mirage is an image of something that looks real, but isn't actually there. Mirages often happen in deserts or on hot road surfaces. You see a patch of blue in the distance that looks like a refreshing pool of water. But when you get closer – it's gone!

HALOES

A halo is a huge ring of light around the Sun, or sometimes the Moon. Haloes are caused by bright sunlight or moonlight shining through crystals of ice in the atmosphere.

▲ Sun haloes look about eight times as wide as the Sun.

MAKING MIRAGES

Mirages can happen when you get layers of air at different temperatures. As light passes between one layer and another, it bends. When light beams from a blue sky pass through cool air into warm air, they are bent upwards. This means blue light appears to be coming from the ground, and our brain is tricked into thinking it is water.

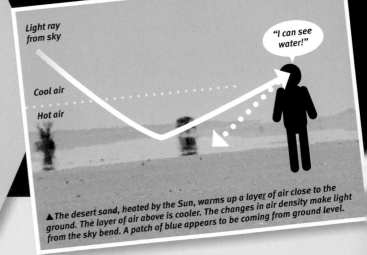

Light ray from sky

"I can see water!"

Cool air

Hot air

▲ The desert sand, heated by the Sun, warms up a layer of air close to the ground. The layer of air above is cooler. The changes in air density make light from the sky bend. A patch of blue appears to be coming from ground level.

AMAZING AURORAS

Auroras are moving patterns of light that sometimes appear in the sky. They happen when particles from the Sun meet the Earth's upper atmosphere. Auroras near the North Pole are called aurora borealis, and those near the South Pole are known as aurora australis.

▼ *The aurora borealis or Northern Lights, seen in northern Canada.*

▲ *Sometimes a Sun halo can appear at the same time as Sun dogs.*

SUN DOGS

Sometimes, as well as a halo, you see two bright spots of light on either side of the Sun. These are known as 'Sun dogs', possibly because they follow the Sun like a dog follows its master.

Animal rain

Strange as it seems, showers of animals really can fall from the sky (see page 62).

Red rain

Sometimes, rain is red – so red that it looks just like blood! (See page 63.)

Strange lightning

There are many kinds of lightning, some a lot stranger than others (see pages 64–65).

Animal rain

When it's raining heavily, people sometimes say "it's raining cats and dogs". But did you know it really can rain animals? Animal rain usually doesn't involve cats and dogs, but fish and frogs have been known to fall from the sky like rain.

FAMOUS CASES

Here are some real-life animal rain reports:

 1873 Thousands of frogs
Kansas City, United States

 1894 Small, jellyfish-like creatures
Bath, United Kingdom

 1947 Fish (minnows and bass)
Marksville, United States

 2009 Tadpoles
Nanao, Japan

 2010 Fish (spangled perch)
Lajamau, Australia

◀ There aren't any good photos of animal rain, but it could look a bit like this!

FISH AND FROGS

Animal rain is rare, but there have been reports of it since ancient times. Many old illustrations show fish and frogs falling from the sky, and occasionally it still happens today. But why? Experts think that sometimes a waterspout sucks up a shoal of fish from the sea, or a tornado sucks up frogs or tadpoles from a pond, and soon afterwards the animals fall back down in a shower.

Red rain

Imagine bright red rain – so red that it looks like blood – falling from the sky! It's a rare event, but it does happen now and again. Luckily, red rain has nothing to do with blood!

RED DUST

Most red rain is caused by winds whipping up reddish dust from desert areas. The dust gets carried into rainclouds, where raindrops condense around the dust particles. If there's a lot of dust, the rain looks red as it falls, and leaves reddish stains behind when it dries up.

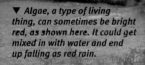

▼ Algae, a type of living thing, can sometimes be bright red, as shown here. It could get mixed in with water and end up falling as red rain.

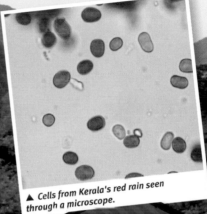

▲ Cells from Kerala's red rain seen through a microscope.

INDIA

Kerala

THE RED RAIN OF KERALA

Red rain fell in Kerala, in southern India, in 2001. Under a microscope, the rain was found to contain tiny reddish cells. Some experts suggested the cells could have come from space, but other scientists say they were the cells of a local type of **algae** found growing on trees, rocks and even lampposts.

Strange lightning

A sizzling hot flash of lightning, crackling with electricity, is one of the wildest types of weather there is – and that's just normal lightning! There are much rarer and stranger types of electrical weather too, such as bizarre lightning balls, ghostly glowing flames and the eerie, electrical effects of earthquakes and volcanoes.

VOLCANIC LIGHTNING

Big flashes of lightning are sometimes seen in the cloud of ash that forms above an erupting volcano. Experts think that particles of air, ash and dust moving around in the cloud build up an electrical charge, as in a thundercloud.

BALLS OF FIRE

Normal lightning happens thousands of times a day around the world, but ball lightning is so rare that most people never see it. It usually appears as a glowing ball of fire that floats through the air during a thunderstorm, burning everything it touches.

▶ *In 1753, a scientist named Georg Richmann was doing an experiment when ball lightning struck him on the head and killed him instantly.*

Ball lightning has been seen to pass right through walls and windows!

ST ELMO'S FIRE

St Elmo's fire is a blue or purple glow that sometimes appears around objects during a storm. It's caused by electrical energy during a storm creating an electric charge that sparks out from something pointed, such as an aircraft's tail or a church tower. In the days of sailing ships, sailors reported seeing the strange glow streaming from the tops of the masts during thunderstorms. They believed it was a good omen that the storm would soon be over. The glow is named after St Elmo, the patron saint of sailors.

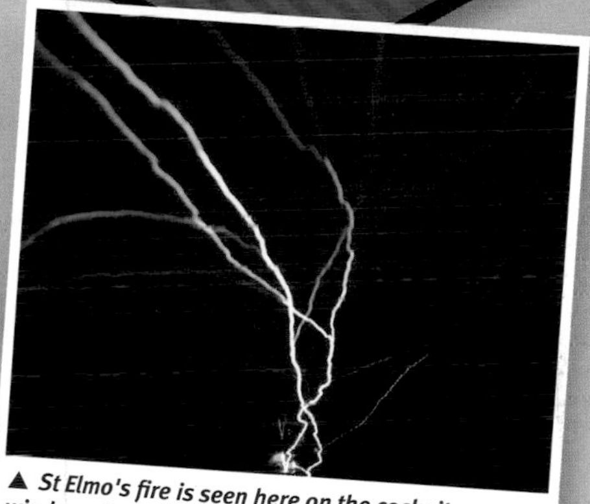

▲ St Elmo's fire is seen here on the cockpit window of an aircraft.

▲ You can clearly see a brilliant flash of volcanic lightning during this eruption in Iceland.

JETS AND SPRITES

Jets and sprites are bursts of coloured lightning that happen high in the atmosphere, up above thunderstorms. They were only discovered in the late 20th century, when they were spotted by high-flying aircraft pilots. Red sprites look like huge jellyfish, while blue jets are narrow and shoot up from the tops of storms.

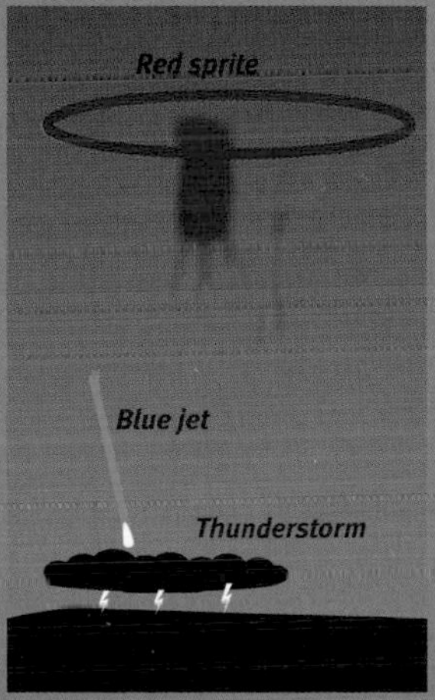

Red sprite

Blue jet

Thunderstorm

Understanding the weather

The science of weather is called **meteorology**. Meteorologists, or weather scientists, don't just study how weather works, they also forecast the weather, predicting what will happen based on the way weather patterns are moving.

▲ A meteorologist launches a weather balloon in Antarctica to collect weather data.

WEATHER FORECASTS

Weather forecasts are made by inputting measurements and other data into computers that turn the information into weather maps. Using special software, forecasters can calculate how the weather patterns will change over the next few days, and where it will be windy, rainy, sunny or snowy.

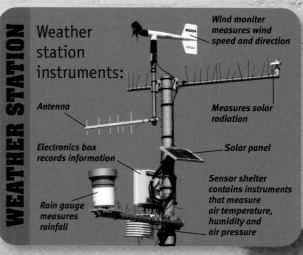

WEATHER STATION

Weather station instruments:

Wind moniter measures wind speed and direction

Antenna

Measures solar radiation

Electronics box records information

Solar panel

Sensor shelter contains instruments that measure air temperature, humidity and air pressure

Rain gauge measures rainfall

Weather maps
Find out what the signs and symbols on weather maps mean (see page 68).

Storm tracking
Find out how forecasters predict where a storm will go (see page 69).

Weather lore
There are many old sayings and beliefs about the weather (see page 70).

WEATHER SCALES

For some types of weather, meteorologists use specially designed weather scales. For example:

 The BEAUFORT SCALE measures wind speed and damage.

The SAFFIR-SIMPSON SCALE measures hurricane intensity.

 The TORRO SCALE measures hailstorm intensity and hailstone size.

 The FUJITA SCALE measures tornado strength and severity.

MEASURING THE WEATHER

To keep track of what the weather is doing, scientists use a range of measuring instruments. As well as taking measurements themselves, they also collect data from automatic weather stations, weather buoys out at sea and weather balloons that are released into the sky. Weather satellites orbiting the Earth also take measurements and photos of weather systems.

▲ *A weather forecaster prepares a weather report using information from lots of different sources.*

▶ *This mobile weather station, installed on sea ice, records many different kinds of weather data.*

Weather satellites

Satellites in space are very useful for watching the weather on Earth (see page 71).

Global warming

The world's climate is getting warmer – find out why here (see page 72).

Energy from the weather

Wind, sun and the water cycle can all give us useful energy (see page 73).

Weather maps

When you watch a weather forecast on TV, you'll usually see the forecaster standing next to a map. The forecaster may show different types of maps of the same place to explain different aspects of the weather.

MORE ON MAPS

As well as using symbols to indicate rain, sunshine and clouds, weather maps use colours to show temperature – green and blue for colder areas, orange and red for warmer weather. Temperatures can also appear in degrees.

WEATHER SYMBOLS

In early TV weather forecasts, forecasters would stick cloud, rain or sunshine stickers onto a map on a wall. Modern TV weather maps are computer-generated, and often animated, but they still use simple symbols for different types of weather.

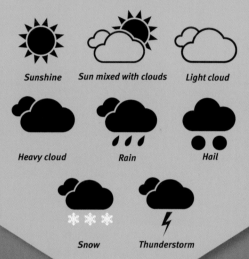

Sunshine	Sun mixed with clouds	Light cloud
Heavy cloud	Rain	Hail
Snow	Thunderstorm	

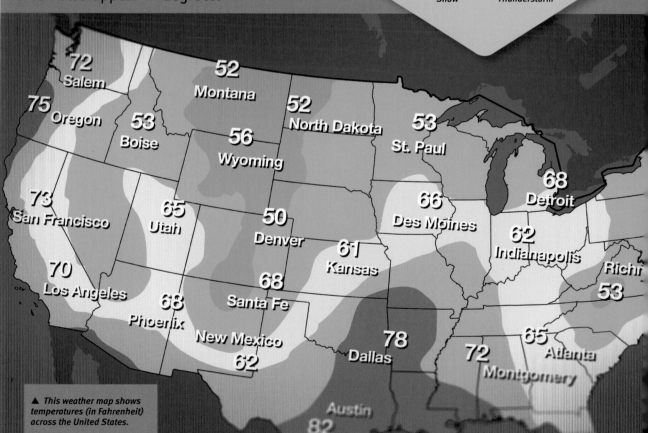

72 Salem
75 Oregon
53 Boise
52 Montana
52 North Dakota
56 Wyoming
53 St. Paul
68 Detroit
73 San Francisco
65 Utah
50 Denver
61 Kansas
66 Des Moines
62 Indianapolis
Richr
53
70 Los Angeles
68 Phoenix
68 Santa Fe
62 New Mexico
78 Dallas
72 Montgomery
65 Atlanta
Austin
82

▲ This weather map shows temperatures (in Fahrenheit) across the United States.

THE CYCLONE'S PATH

As a tropical cyclone moves across the ocean, scientists use data from satellites and weather stations to track it and predict its path over the next few days. Cyclones can move in a straight line or a gentle curve. Sometimes they change direction. This depends on the following four things:

- The location, size and speed of the storm itself
- Other winds in the area
- Areas of high or low pressure in the area
- The way the Earth spins

Storm tracking

It's always useful to know what the weather will be like tomorrow – especially if a gigantic storm is heading your way! When a big tropical cyclone, such as a typhoon, is detected over an ocean, forecasters track it very carefully so they can predict when and where it will hit land.

▲ *This satellite image shows the huge and powerful Typhoon Hagupit rapidly approaching the Philippines.*

▲ *After hearing an advance storm warning, people in the Philippines rush to an evacuation centre to escape the strong winds and heavy rain of Typhoon Hagupit.*

▲ *Map showing the path of Typhoon Hagupit.*

STORM WARNING!

When a powerful storm is approaching land, weather warnings are broadcast to let people know that the storm is on its way. This gives them time to board up their houses, evacuate the area or get to a storm shelter. When Typhoon Hagupit finally made landfall in the Philippines on 6 December 2014, the advance warnings saved many lives.

Before weather stations, satellites and forecasting software were invented, people predicted the weather in other ways. They looked at the colours and patterns of clouds, and even at how animals behaved. But were they right to? There are lots of old weather sayings and proverbs – and some do seem to come true!

COWS AND RAIN

People say that when cows lie down, rain is on the way! Is this true? Scientists think that cows stand up in hot weather to cool their undersides, and lie down when it's colder. Cold weather often brings rain, so the saying could be true!

PINE CONE PREDICTOR

Some types of pine cones close up when there is water in the air, and open when it's dry – so pine cones can help to predict rainy weather!

Closed cone, damp weather   *Open cone, dry weather*

◀ *This spectacular sunset has turned the whole sky red – which could mean good weather!*

RED SKIES

Red sky at night, shepherd's delight.

Red sky in the morning, shepherd's warning.

This can be true if you live in a place such as Europe, where weather systems mainly come from the west. Reddish sunsets and sunrises are caused by dust particles in dry, warm air. A red sunset means the dusty air is in the west and moving towards you, so fine weather is coming. A red sunrise means the good weather is in the east, so has probably already passed by.

MOON RING

A ring around the Moon means rain upon you soon.

A ring around the Moon is caused by ice crystals in the air. Ice crystals can sink lower and form rain clouds, so there's some truth in the saying.

Weather satellites

Satellites are objects that orbit our planet. Humans have sent many types of satellites into orbit. Some are used to study the stars, some carry internet signals, and others monitor the weather on the Earth by watching it from above.

Solar panels provide electrical power.

▼ Meteosat is a typical weather satellite. Its instruments scan the Earth for tropical storms and other weather events.

A transmitter sends data to receivers on the Earth.

Sunshades shield the detecting telescopes and cameras.

▲ This Meteosat weather satellite image shows the weather systems over Europe and Africa.

WEATHER MONITOR

Weather satellites usually make images of the Earth that can reveal weather patterns. They have cameras that sense the same kind of light that we can see, and infra-red sensors that detect heat. Some also have extra-sensitive light sensors that can spot lightning, forest fires and volcanic eruptions.

▲ A weather satellite image of snow and snow clouds covering Ireland.

Global warming

In the past, the Earth has been both much hotter and much colder than it is now. But over the last century, scientists have found that it is heating up unusually fast – a condition known as global warming.

WATERY WORLD

Global warming is melting the world's ice. As the glaciers and ice sheets around the poles shrink, the meltwater flows into the sea, making sea levels rise. In the last 100 years, sea levels have risen by 20 centimetres, and they are still rising.

▲ A huge chunk of ice breaks off a glacier in Argentina.

▶ This burning gas is adding more greenhouse gases to the atmosphere.

THE CAUSE

Scientists think that current global warming is caused by pollution. When we burn fossil fuels, such as coal, oil and natural gas, we add 'greenhouse gases', including carbon dioxide, to the air. These gases help to trap heat in the Earth's atmosphere, in the same way that a greenhouse traps heat under its glass roof.

THE EFFECTS

Global warming affects the planet in the following ways:

* Increased temperatures
* Rising sea levels
* Changes in weather, such as more lightning and stronger hurricanes
* Changes in bird migration patterns
* Shrinking ice caps and glaciers
* Decrease in numbers of polar animals such as walruses and polar bears

Energy from the weather

Humans burn fossil fuels for heating, to power vehicles and to generate electricity. This makes waste gases that are thought to contribute to global warming. Eventually, however, fossil fuels will run out, so people are developing ways of collecting energy from other sources, including the weather.

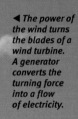

◀ The power of the wind turns the blades of a wind turbine. A generator converts the turning force into a flow of electricity.

RENEWABLE ENERGY

Energy can be produced from different types of weather, such as wind, sunshine or rushing water. Because these energy sources will never run out, they are called **renewable energy** sources. Producing energy from the weather creates less pollution – and less global warming – than getting our energy from fossil fuels.

▼ Solar cells contain materials that turn sunlight into electricity.

▲ Hydroelectric power stations use energy from water flowing downhill.

Weather records

MOST EXTREME TORNADO

Tri-State Tornado, Missouri, Illinois and Indiana, United States, 18 March 1925 –
• longest path length at 352 kilometres
• longest lasting at 3.5 hours
• fastest forward speed for a big tornado at 117 kilometres per hour.

DEEPEST SNOWFALL

Tamarack, California, United States, January 1911 – 1145 centimetres.

FASTEST WIND

Oklahoma, United States, 3 May 1999 – 512 kilometres per hour, in a tornado.

SUNNIEST PLACE

Yuma, Arizona, United States – about 4020 hours of sunshine per year.

BIGGEST RAINDROPS

Over Brazil and the Pacific Ocean – one centimetre.

DRIEST PLACE

Atacama Desert, Chile – some parts never receive rainfall.

TEMPERATURE SCALES

There are two main scales for measuring weather temperature: the Celsius (also known as Centigrade) scale and the Fahrenheit scale.

Hottest weather temperature

Coldest weather temperature

Equator

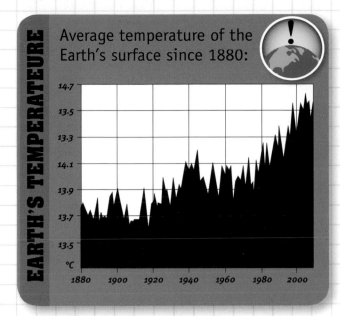

EARTH'S TEMPERATURE

Average temperature of the Earth's surface since 1880:

14.7
13.5
13.3
14.1
13.9
13.7
13.5
°C

1880 1900 1920 1940 1960 1980 2000

COLDEST TEMPERATURE
Vostok research station, Antarctica, 21 July 1983 – -89.2°C.

COLDEST AVERAGE TEMPERATURE
East Antarctic Polar Plateau – average temperature -56.4°C.

HOTTEST TEMPERATURE
Death Valley, Arizona, United States, 10 July 1913 – 56.7°C.

HOTTEST AVERAGE TEMPERATURE FOR AN INHABITED PLACE
Dallol, Ethiopia – average temperature 34.4°C.

MOST DEADLY FLOODS
Central China floods, 1931 – killed up to 3.7 million people.

WETTEST PLACE
Mawsynram, India – average rainfall 11,872 millimetres per year.

MOST DEADLY STORM
Bhola cyclone, hit what was East Pakistan (now Bangladesh), 12 November 1970 – killed up to half a million people.

Antarctica

Great weather scientists

Ancient Greek scientist Aristotle (384–322 BCE) was one of the first people to study the weather in detail. In his book, *Meteorology*, he described several types of weather, such as lightning, clouds, tornadoes and frost, and explained how the water cycle works.

DO IT YOURSELF!

If you'd like to be a meteorologist, it will help if you choose subjects such as geography, maths and sciences.

Ancient Egyptians believed that the Sun sailed across the sky in a shallow boat.

Pliny the Elder

Pliny the Elder (23–79 CE)
The Roman naturalist Pliny wrote a work called *Natural History*, which included detailed explanations of different kinds of weather.

Daniel Gabriel Fahrenheit

Daniel Gabriel Fahrenheit (1686–1736)
Fahrenheit was a German engineer who developed new designs for thermometers, and invented the Fahrenheit temperature scale.

Anders Celsius

Anders Celsius (1701–1744)
Celsius was a Swedish astronomer. He realised that auroras were linked to the Earth's magnetic field, and developed the Centigrade or Celsius scale.

Benjamin Franklin

Benjamin Franklin (1706–1790)
Franklin was an American politician and scientist. He showed that lightning is made of electricity, and invented the lightning rod or conductor.

Georg Richmann

Georg Richmann (1711–1753)
This German scientist studied temperature, evaporation and electric storms, and is said to have been killed by ball lightning.

John Dalton

John Dalton (1766–1844)
Dalton, an English scientist, studied the atmosphere and the gases it contains, made charts of weather data and invented weather instruments.

Luke Howard

Luke Howard (1772–1864)
Howard was an English chemist and meteorologist who studied different types of clouds and developed a cloud naming system that is still used today.

Alfred Wegener

Alfred Wegener (1880–1930)
German scientist Alfred Wegener studied weather at the poles and high in the Earth's atmosphere. He was the first to use kites and balloons to collect weather data.

Coching Chu

Coching Chu (1890-1974)
Chinese meteorologist Coching Chu was one of China's leading scientists. He is best-known for his work studying typhoons.

Joanne Malkus Simpson

Joanne Malkus Simpson (1923–2010)
US scientist Joanne Simpson is famous for her studies of tropical clouds, thunderstorms and hurricanes, and was a chief weather researcher for NASA.

Warren Washington

Warren Washington (born 1936)
US scientist Warren Washington is a leading authority on the atmosphere, and is known for his work using computers to model the Earth's climate.

James Hansen

James Hansen (born 1941)
US scientist James Hansen is famous for his studies of the atmosphere and climate change, and his campaigns to combat global warming.

Christiana Figueres

Christiana Figueres (born 1956)
Costa Rican diplomat and campaigner Christiana Figueres is a leading UN official working in the area of climate change and renewable energy.

GLOSSARY

ALGAE
A type of living thing, a bit like a plant, that is often found in water.

ATMOSPHERE
The layer of gases surrounding the Earth, in which our weather takes place.

BLACKOUT
A loss of electricity supply to an area, which can be caused by storms, floods or high winds damaging power cables.

CELL
A large-scale, rotating pattern of air movement in the atmosphere.

CLIMATE
The typical or normal weather conditions found in a particular place.

CLIMATE CHANGE
A long-term change in the climate of the Earth, or of a particular area.

DOLDRUMS
An area of the Atlantic Ocean close to the Equator where there is often a lack of wind.

FAMINE
A severe, long-term food shortage that can cause starvation.

FOSSIL FUEL
A natural fuel, such as coal or oil, formed long ago from the remains of living things.

FRONT
The front edge of a moving mass of air that can be warm or cold. The movements of weather fronts help forecasters to predict the weather.

FROSTBITE
Damage to parts of the body, such as the nose, toes and fingers, caused by very cold temperatures.

GLOBAL WARMING
A gradual increase in the Earth's average temperatures, measured during the 20th and 21st centuries.

GREENHOUSE GASES
A group of gases found in the atmosphere, such as carbon dioxide and methane, that absorbs heat and contributes to global warming.

HEAT ISLAND
An area such as a city, where human activities such as heating homes make the temperature warmer than in the surrounding area.

HEMISPHERE
One of the two halves of the Earth that meet at the Equator. North of the Equator is the northern hemisphere, and south of it is the southern hemisphere.

HUMIDITY
The amount of water, in the form of water vapour, carried in the air. In very humid weather, the air feels damp.

ICE AGE
A long period of time when the Earth's average temperature is very low, and large areas are covered by ice.

METEOROLOGY
The study of the atmosphere, weather and weather forecasting.

MILLIBARS
Units of air pressure that show how much the Earth's atmosphere is pressing down on the Earth at a particular time and place.

MOONBOW
A faint rainbow caused by bright moonlight instead of sunshine.

PRECIPITATION
Any kind of weather that involves water coming out of the atmosphere and falling to the ground – for example, rain, sleet, snow or hail.

PREVAILING WIND
The most common wind direction found in a particular place.

RAIN SHADOW
An area that does not receive much rain because a barrier of mountains prevents rain clouds from blowing over it.

RENEWABLE ENERGY
Energy from a source that doesn't get used up, such as wind power.

SMOG
A mixture of fog and smoke or other pollution. It can cause breathing problems for some people.

SUPERCELL
A big, powerful stormcloud that can lead to thunderstorms or tornadoes.

TEMPERATE
Weather, temperature or climate that is mild and not extreme. Temperate regions are usually found about half way between the poles and the Equator.

TRADE WIND
A wind blowing almost constantly towards the Equator from the east.

TROPICAL
Weather, temperature or climate in the Tropics – the areas close to the Equator. The Tropics are often warm and damp.

TROPICAL CYCLONE
A large, powerful, whirling windstorm, which can be known as a hurricane, cyclone or typhoon, depending on where it forms.

WATER VAPOUR
Water in the form of a gas, which is carried in the atmosphere.

WHITEOUT
A combination of thickly falling snow and wind that makes everything appear totally white.

INDEX